Dear Loneliness

By: Aaron Fields

ISBN: 978-1-953962-13-3

CONTENTS

<u>Something To Think About Before You Read</u>

"Loneliness is one of the most pervasive and well-known issues taking place in society today."

----------*Aaron Fields*

Word From The Author

Why are most people in this world suffering from loneliness? Is it because we no longer value ourselves? Is it because we don't have a code of ethics or a set of standards to adhere to? Do you think it's because we don't know who we are? Is it because we don't understand our purpose in life? Is it because we don't have a support system? Is it because we live in a dysfunctional society? Or is it all the above?

It is apparent that because of the dysfunction of this "civilized society", many people are walking around looking like zombies. It seems like this society is attempting to dismantle any form of connection between men and women, causing them to suffer in silence. Most people in this society are facing psychological, identity and spiritual issues, even depression.

Yes, feeling down and discouraged when things are not going well is inevitable. However, loneliness is problematic when it leads to depression, negative self-image, or self-destructive behavior. Depending on how much you're struggling, your condition could hinder your ability to function on a daily basis, which includes school, work, or personal life.

Can Loneliness Affect Your Health?

Is there a link between loneliness and your health? Yes, because your way of thinking can affect your physical body. The way how you feel on the inside can affect your outward appearance.

If you are suffering from loneliness and its affecting your health, take time to assess why you feel this way. Yes, one can argue that feeling sad and lonely is to be expected. However, when these feelings last for an extended period, it becomes an immense problem. Why? Well, it's because it can interfere with your ability to function in this society.

Perhaps it may be time to change your situation. Do you need to find a group of trusted individuals to confide in? Can you find a safe way to express yourself? How often do you workout? Are you getting enough sleep? Do you eat healthy? Do you read inspirational materials or pray? Depending on what you decide to do, always keep in mind that the goal is to remain healthy and stable in every aspect of your life.

Does The World Want You To Be Lonely?

It's important to understand that the antidepressant industry and medication field is a business. All they care about is the money. These industries need you to be lonely. Most of the people in these industries don't care about your overall health and well-being. Hypothetically speaking, if these industries were to address the issues of loneliness, it'll only be because it will provide them with a payout.

Why do they want you to be lonely? Well, because when you're lonely, you become desperate. When you become desperate, you lose sight of who you are. When you lose sight of who you are, you can't control yourself. When you can't control yourself, you become more susceptible to drugs and alcohol. When you rely on drugs and alcohol, or anything that's self-destructive, it can lead to death, injuries, prison, and court cases, which leads to more money. Speaking of court cases, the judicial field is a multibillion dollar industry as well. Are you noticing the pattern? Everyone is trying to get paid off of someone's dysfunction.

Do You Feel Lonely?

Why do you feel lonely? Is it because you never had a moral framework? Is it because you never learned how to conduct yourself? I think it's fair to say that most people never had a set of customs or a code of ethics to go by. When people don't have a set of laws and rules to abide by, they become chaotic and confused.

To grow up in a functional society, there must be order, law, and structure, not chaos and confusion. Do you think it's important to have a strong culture? Do you think it's important to know right from wrong? Is it important to celebrate certain customs and traditions based on your family structure? Unfortunately, these are the things you don't see in society that often because everybody wants to do their own thing. This explains why most of you feel lonely and left out.

Why do you feel left out? Is it because you can't relate to anyone? Most of us can feel excluded because of the society's poor communication between men and women and adults and children. Think about it, sometimes when a child gets to a certain age, the parents can no longer keep that line of communication open. Unfortunately, many parents are not encouraging their children to ask questions. In most cases, a lot of parents don't want to humble themselves and take the time to listen to what their children have to say. When you choose to dismiss your child's questions and comments, you can't get mad and upset when they look for answers in other places. Keep in mind, not everyone has good intentions for your children. Another major thing that makes communication poor in this society has a lot to do with the infatuation people have with the internet and social media. Some individuals attempt to fabricate a false image or cultivate a cult of personality to glorify themselves.

Do You Lack Companionship?

It doesn't surprise me that most people lack companionship. If a society is trying to start a gender war, do you think this will lead to "healthy companionships"? No, it wouldn't because telling women that men are their enemies will not help. Teaching men how to hate or worship women is problematic.

It's important for people to understand that men and women are supposedto complement one another, not fight and hate on each other. Unfortunately, this society teaches men and women to compete and argue with one another. Between both genders, the ultimate goal is to gain a psychological advantage over the other person.

Why do you think some of these work environments are so toxic? Why is the atmosphere so negative? Not only do gender wars take place on social media, but they also occur in Corporate America (workplace). Many people in the workspace have a hidden agenda to sabotage and provoke other people. Why is that? It's because most toxic individuals come from chaotic households. Due to their upbringing and the toxic ideologies they became privy to, they carry the negative ideas over into the work environment.

Unfortunately, a lot of women will not develop a healthy and successful relationship with other men because they don't respect the idea of manhood. Sadly, most men will not develop a fulfilling relationship with women because they don't love or understand the essence of womanhood. As a man, it's very important to understand the nature of the woman, and respect the feminine gender. The man has to know how to love the woman so that way he won't diminish the feminine principle. However, men shouldn't worship the woman either. One major issue we're having in this society is that too many men are obsessed with women. Because of the men's lack of understanding regarding women, they try to overcompensate by seeking women's validation. In addition to that, men also take extreme measures by committing wicked and immoral acts towards women. In other words, many men put too much of their time and energy into women as opposed to working on themselves (mentally, financially, emotionally, and spiritually).

Difference Between Loneliness & Being Alone

Believe it or not, there is a difference between being lonely and being alone. A person who is lonely feels that lack of human interaction, and as a result, they need that energy from another person in order to continue to move forward in life. People who are alone understand that they must learn how to deal with certain issues in their life without being able to count on anyone else.

There is nothing wrong with being alone. Why? Well, because sometimes in life it's necessary to be alone, especially if you want to succeed in life. Don't be afraid to achieve your goals in life. A major reason most people fear success is because they understand they may have to embrace solitude for an extended period.

Most people don't realize they have to complete certain life objectives on their own without the aid of other people to succeed. It's very rare that you're going to have a group of people enduring the hardships of life with you. If you want to start a business, you might have to start one on your own. If you want to be great at something or learn how to monetize your gifts, be willing to work hard by yourself. You must know how to be alone without being lonely.

Are Your Ideas Being Shared With Others?

Are you struggling with sharing your ideas and interests with other people? Are your ideas getting rejected? Are you relying on the validation of others? If so, it sounds like you need to work on getting more comfortable in your own skin. It is imperative that you become more confident in yourself and develop a high self-esteem.

Please understand that not everyone will like you or your ideas. Why? It's because that's part of life and you have to deal with it. There is nothing wrong with moving on with your life and with your own ideas. Just make sure that your ideas and interests are not illegal, and make sure they don't conflict with the laws of God and the laws of the land.

If people don't share your ideas and your interests, that's okay. You know why? It's because when your ideas come to fruition and your dreams become a reality, that's when people are going to show up. In order for anything in your life to get accomplished, you need to believe in yourself and have the desire to be a better person each day. You must have a healthy image of yourself because if you have a poor self image, you're going to rely on other people to make you happy. You must tell yourself who you are and don't allow other people to tell you who you are.

Something To Keep In Mind

People who seek attention by behaving chaotically and ranting about unfamiliar topics on social media are probably experiencing loneliness. Why is that? It's because these kinds of people don't even believe half the things they talk about. They just want to see if they can get you to believe in the nonsense they subscribe to.

The difference between a confident person and an individual who blusters is that the person who is confident will always be sure of themselves and their abilities. The individual who blusters are just loudmouths who seek attention but never a solution to a problem. This explains why their personal lives are in disarray.

Nothing Wrong With Following The Old Path

Although change is inevitable, change is not always a good thing. Why? Well, because change can be costly, stressful, destructive, and risky. Before making a change, we may need to remember where we come from to stay grounded.

There is nothing wrong with sticking to the old path. What do I mean by that? For example, a man presiding over his family is important. When I say a man presiding over his family, I don't mean it in a demeaning way because a man should never belittle the woman or the children. In fact, the man should honor them because having substantial power comes with great leadership and responsibility. In other words, the man should never abuse his power. His job is to be a safety net for the family. A man should never intentionally bring negativity and instability into the woman's life or in the child's life.

Desperate and impulsive decisions are often the result of depression and loneliness. Unfortunately, most of these people that make poor decisions can never comprehend why they're lonely and depressed. Believe it or not, most people in this society need a lot of help. Unfortunately, those who set the standards and norms of society want people to be lonely and depressed, making it hard for them to get the help they require. As I mentioned earlier in this book, there is a lot of money involved in being lonely and depressed. This society does not want people to go back to having stability. The influence of your

surrounding culture can make you unaware of the danger you're in.

What About Marriage?

Why do you think more people are choosing to get married at a much later age? Why do you think other people are choosing to not get married at all? Is it because there's a lack of trust? How do you describe marriage in today's society? In the current society we live in today, marriage is more of a contractual agreement. Unfortunately, marriage is no longer abouta spiritual union. Therefore, without a spiritual union, it becomes that much harder to create a cultural framework within the family system.

For those that don't want to get married in this current society we're in, I understand where you're coming from. Most men and women no longer trust one another, so if you are someone that's planning on getting married, please be very careful and use a methodical approach. Just because you sign a marriage contract and have a beautiful wedding ceremony doesn't mean your marriage will last.

In relationships, both individuals need to be capable of dealing with monotony. What do I mean by monotony? It's important for both people to recognize that routines can often be consistent, predictable, and repetitive. Are you willing to accept monotony in your relationship? Is this something you can handle? Are you mature enough to comprehend that a lot of things in your relationships are going to be repetitive? Please understand that being in a relationship involves accepting monotony. Most people have trouble understanding this concept. They believe everything in the relationship has to be new and spontaneous every single day; otherwise they'll get bored and end the relationship. If you're not willing to accept monotony, then you should not seek marriage or a serious relationship.

It is apparent in today's society that many people are getting married for the wrong reasons. Sadly, those involved in such relationships neglect to investigate their partner thoroughly. Another reason most of these relationships never work is because one or both parties never took the time to get to know themselves first. It's difficult to understand yourself as a person when you don't value yourself. Nowadays, people marry based on their emotions, impulses, and momentary needs.

Women are forced to depend on external entities and societal frameworks for protection due to toxic ideologies and male negligence. As a result, this makes marriage less relevant.

The purpose of marriage is to have both gender roles complement one another. In this current society, you have both men and women fighting and arguing with each other. This is because most women no longer respect male authority. As it pertains to men, most of them are being conditioned to worship or hate women. These types of teachings go against the essential nature of both men and women.

Can Dysfunction Lead To Loneliness & Depression?

Most people in this society don't understand that suffering from loneliness and depression is a recipe for disaster. In life, it's easier to obfuscate people than to enlighten them. Why are most people in society confused? When you don't know who you are and you don't know where you're going, it's easy to get manipulated.

When you allow other people to obfuscate the main issue in your life, you no longer have a set of standards to go by. You can no longer distinguish between right and wrong. When you accept any kind of change in your life, it will lead to a lot of confusion and unnecessary problems. It's hard to create a set of standards for yourself when you don't know who you are. When someone leaves behind their customary values, beliefs,culture, and identity, it can cause them to feel isolated and hopeless.

Activity: Tell me a few things about your culture. What are some of your customs? What kinds of principles and standards does your culture abide by? What do you value most about yourself?

_____

_____

_____

_____

_____

_____

_____

_____

_____

_____

_____

_____

_____

_____

_____

_____

Don't Fall Into Depression

It's important to understand that a person can experience a lot of mental and physical health issues because of prolong periods of loneliness. In addition to that, depression can result from loneliness. That's why it's important to take the time to assess your situation and figure out why are you feeling down and depressed.

To alleviate feelings of loneliness and depression, it's necessary to concentrate on positive thoughts that can elevate your existence in society. If you choose to not focus on productivity and not strive to become the best version of yourself, you can fall into the state loneliness and depression.

Sometimes in life, human beings spend too much time focusing on things that are no longer relevant. Did you break up with someone that you were in a relationship with? Did you get fired from your job? Are you fearful that you may not get married or have children in the future? Whatever it is, it's important that you pull yourself together and have some level of control over your mind. Too many people are obsessed with things that have nothing to do with their purpose on the earth. Rather than aiming to better ourselves, many of us are weighed down with negative ideas that are polluting our minds. Having a polluted mind can lead to feeling less valued and having a poor self-image.

What causes depression? Is depression caused by biological and genetic factors? Is there a psychological factor that contributes to depression? Is it fair to assume that a contributing factor to loneliness and depression has a lot to do with the different ideologies that are being taught by society that lead to people feeling dissatisfied and unfulfilled?

What Are You Doing Wrong?

If you're feeling lonely, does that mean you have internal issues that need to be addressed? Well, it's possible because sometimes in life we need to look at ourselves in the mirror. If you're constantly running into the same issues, maybe you're the problem. There is nothing wrong with humbling yourself and reflecting on some things that you're doing wrong.

Are you partaking in self-destructive behavior? Are you setting unrealistic expectations for yourself? Are you pushing good people out of your life? Are you bringing negative people into your life? Whatever it is, it may be in your best interest to omit the toxic things out of your life, especially when dealing with negative people.

One of the best things you can do for yourself in this world is to remove the toxicity out of your life, especially if you're trying to develop a peaceful mind. Sadly, there are so many people that continue to put themselves in dangerous and uncomfortable situations with toxic people. It's important to know when it's necessary to cut someone out of your life. The moment you come across a person who is a negative person, draining, and destructive with nothing to lose, make sure you get them out of your life as soon as possible. Why? Well, because they will attempt to ruin your life if you let them. Please understand that misery loves company. Some people are so miserable and lonely that the only satisfaction they get in life is from watching others suffer. Knowing when and how to keep positive people in your support system is crucial as they bring irreplaceable value to your life. Always remember to not take good people for granted, especially if they treat you with love and respect.

Final Message

If you are lonely, it's most likely because you're not doing a good enough job of establishing healthy standards for yourself. It's also likely that you still haven't figured out your purpose in life. Please understand that whether you're a man or a woman, always pursue the things that will create a better life for you.

Of course, you must keep in mind that whatever goals you have written on your list, pursue them with passion. Loneliness can cause individuals to have unrealistic expectations for themselves. Unfortunately, many individuals get fixated on getting married, having kids, getting a house, or getting a certain level of income by a certain age. Although these are great goals to have, what happens if you're not married by age twenty-eight? What happens when you don't have children by age thirty? What happens when you don't have your house by age thirty-two?

The overall point I'm trying to make is that you can't live your life with the assumption that you're going to achieve something at a certain age. Not saying that setting goals is a bad thing, but sometimes in life, certain things come at a much later time. All you can do is remain patient and continue to set goals for yourself. Have you ever tried developing a healthy spiritual connection with God? If so, I encourage you to try it because that's going to prevent you from being too concerned with other people and how society views you. You can't worry about how other people value you because you have to value and love yourself first. It is apparent that we, as human beings, are interdependent creatures. A society built on the notion of individualism, self-adulation, and a lack of a powerful community can cause an increase in mental breakdowns. Why? Well, it's because people are not getting the love and satisfaction that they're supposed to be getting from their community. Loneliness can become chronic if not dealt with effectively. Hence, it is essential to handle loneliness in healthy ways to limit the likelihood of developing more long-term issues. Always remember that there are measures you can take to prevent loneliness and depression.

Notes

END

www.ingramcontent.com/pod-product-compliance
Lightning Source LLC
Chambersburg PA
CBHW081640040426
42449CB00014B/3395